Making Choices
for a HEALTHY BODY

By Diane Lindsey Reeves

21st Century Junior Library

Published in the United States of America by
Cherry Lake Publishing
Ann Arbor, Michigan
www.cherrylakepublishing.com

Reading Adviser: Marla Conn MS. Ed., Literacy specialist, Read-Ability, Inc.

Photo Credits: Cover, © wavebreakmedia; page 4, © Africa Studio; page 6, © Monkey Business Images; page 8, © Cheryl Casey; page 10, © Blend Images; page 12, © Sergey Novikov; page 14, © Pressmaster; page 16, © antoniodiaz; page 18, © Soloviova Liudmyla; page 20, © Monkey Business Images. *Source: Shutterstock.*

Copyright © 2018 by Cherry Lake Publishing
All rights reserved. No part of this book may be reproduced or utilized in any form or by any means without written permission from the publisher.

Library of Congress Cataloging-in-Publication Data
Names: Reeves, Diane Lindsey, 1959- author.
Title: Making choices for a healthy body / by Diane Lindsey Reeves.
Description: Ann Arbor, Mich. : Cherry Lake Publishing, [2018] | Series: Smart choices | Audience: K to grade 3. | Includes bibliographical references and index.
Identifiers: LCCN 2017035919 | ISBN 9781534107908 (hardcover) | ISBN 9781534109889 (pdf) | ISBN 9781534108899 (pbk.) | ISBN 9781534120877 (hosted ebook)
Subjects: LCSH: Health behavior—Juvenile literature. | Decision making—Juvenile literature.
Classification: LCC RA776.9 .R432 2018 | DDC 613—dc23
LC record available at https://lccn.loc.gov/2017035919

Cherry Lake Publishing would like to acknowledge the work of The Partnership for 21st Century Skills. Please visit *www.p21.org* for more information.

Printed in the United States of America.

CONTENTS

5 **Hello, Me**

13 **Move It**

19 **Stay Safe**

22 My Smart Choices

23 Glossary

24 Index

24 About the Author

Every person is one of a kind.

Hello, Me

Lucky you. You get to be you! You are one of a kind. There is no one else in the world exactly like you.

How can you be the best *you*? By taking good care of yourself. By doing all you can to be **healthy** and happy.

In this book, you will have choices. Think about how to be the very best *you*.

My Choice!

- Take good care of myself
- Don't take good care of myself

Healthy foods come from nature.

What is one of the best ways to be healthy? Eat healthy foods! There are so many choices!

Healthy bodies need lots of good food choices. Fruits and vegetables. Milk, cheese, and other dairy foods. **Proteins** from meats, beans, and nuts. **Grains** like cereal and bread.

All these foods have different jobs to do. They work together to keep your body healthy and strong.

My Choice!

- Eat different kinds of food
- Eat whatever I want

Drinking plenty of water keeps your body healthy.

More than half of your body is made up of water. Did you know that? It's true. Your body needs lots of water to work properly.

Your body must work harder when you don't drink enough water. You get thirsty. It means you get tired. You can't do your best thinking. You might even get a **headache**.

Juice and other drinks are okay as a treat once in awhile. But your body needs, water, water, water!

My Choice!

- Drink lots of water
- Drink juice and soda instead

Healthy bodies need plenty of sleep.

There is so much to do every day. Sometimes you don't want to go to bed. Just one more game! Just one more book!

Your body needs sleep to stay healthy. Your body had a busy day! It needs to **recover**. A good night of rest help it get strong and grow bigger.

Experts say that kids like you need lots of sleep. Nine to 11 hours each night is best. Are you getting enough sleep each night?

My Choice!

- Get to bed on time
- Stay up as late as I can

Exercise can be lots of fun.

Move It

Healthy bodies need fresh air and **exercise**. You get exercise in your PE class at school. But that's not the only way to get **fit**.

Get outside and get moving! Ride your bike or play chase. Walk in the park with your family. What is the secret to staying fit? Find things you like to do. Then do them as much as you can!

My Choice!

- Get out and move
- Sit around and do nothing

Sports are a great way to get exercise.

Playing sports helps keep you healthy. It's a great way to make new friends. And it's fun!

There are so many sports to choose from. T-ball and softball. Basketball and soccer. Tennis, swimming, and **martial arts**.

Sports **challenge** you to try new things. You might even surprise yourself. You might do things you didn't think you could do.

Now you have to answer one question. Which sport do you want to play?

My Choice!

- Join a sports team
- Play video games

Many children enjoy learning to play musical instruments.

There are other ways to stay healthy. Do things you enjoy!

You can get involved in something. Join a club. Join a scouting group. Take a cooking class. Do art or act in a play.

You might even want to start a new **hobby**. Plant a garden or start a collection.

What kinds of things do you like to do? Fun activities help us **relax**. They give our brains a break.

My Choice!

- Try out new activities
- Do the same old things I always do

Buckle up, everyone! It's time to stay safe.

Stay Safe

There are some things you always do to stay safe. You buckle your seat belt every time you ride in a car. You wear a helmet every time you ride a bike. You always look both ways before you cross the street.

There are some things you should never do What unsafe things should you avoid?

My Choice!

- Be careful about safety
- Do whatever I want to do

Enjoying time with your family is a healthy thing to do.

A healthy you is a happy you. You have the **energy** to do things you enjoy. You have the brain power to do well in school. You feel good and look your best.

Take good care of your body. That way, you are taking good care of you! What kind of healthy choices will you make today?

My Choice!
- Make healthy choices
- Make unhealthy choices

MY SMART CHOICES

Write a story about two different days. One day you make smart choices for a healthy body. The other day you don't. How are the two days different? Which day did you enjoy the most?

GLOSSARY

challenge (CHAL-inj) to interest someone by daring them to do something that takes extra effort

energy (EN-ur-jee) the ability or strength to do things without getting tired

exercise (EK-sur-size) physical activity that you do to stay strong and healthy

fit (FIT) to be strong and healthy

grains (GRAYNZ) foods made from crops such as wheat, corn, rice, oats, and barley

headache (HED-ake) an ache or pain in your head

healthy (HEL-thee) strong and not likely to get sick; also, something that is good for your body, such as food

hobby (HAH-bee) something you enjoy doing when you have free time

martial arts (MAHR-shuhl AHRTS) a sport of self-defense

proteins (PROH-teerz) things in food that make your body strong

relax (ri-LAKS) to take a rest from work or to do something enjoyable

recover (ree-KUHV-ur) to get better after a hard time

INDEX

B
beans, 7
bread, 7

C
cereal, 7
cheese, 7

E
exercise, 12, 13

F
fruits, 7

G
grains, 7

H
headache, 7
hobby, 17

M
martial arts, 15
milk, 7

N
nuts, 7

P
protein, 7

S
seatbelt, 19

sleep, 11
soccer, 15
softball, 15
sports, 15
swimming, 15

T
T-ball, 15
tennis, 15

V
vegetables, 7

W
water, 7

ABOUT THE AUTHOR

When Diane Lindsey Reeves isn't writing children's books, she chooses to play with her four grandchildren. She lives in Cary, North Carolina and Washington, D.C.